LLAMAS
&
ALPACAS
as a
METAPHOR
for
LIFE
2nd edition

D1404399

written by
Marty McGee Bennett

photography by
Sandy Flanagan
(unless otherwise noted)

Library of Congress Card Catalog Number: 2001117087

ISBN: 0-9709916-5-7

First Printing 1996

Printed in the United States of America.

Published by
Raccoon Press
Dundee, NY & Bend, OR
racoonpress@camelidynamics.com
www.camelidynamics.com
800.570.LAMA

RaccoonPress
bend, oregon

Front cover photo by
Su Lenk, AzSu Alpacas,
Thetford, Norfolk, England

Line drawings by
B.J. Lewis

Inside front cover photo by
Cindy Efinger

FOR MY GRANDMOTHER
JOSEPHINE STONEBURNER

This book is dedicated to all of the people over the years that have hosted clinics. Wonderful people, who have invited me into their homes and their barns and taken a chance on my ability to make it a good show. Thank you for your faith in me and your commitment to the animals.

Be hard to leave.

Llamas and alpacas as a methaphor for life...What does that mean? So often when I am traveling, visiting or teaching a clinic, the conversation revolves around animals and the magic they bring to our lives. We are very different from animals and yet so much the same. I feel that as soon as I was ready to listen and learn, the animals in my life became some of my most important teachers. Somehow I could see myself in the animal mirror and learn more easily from them than from my fellow humans.

In the years since the 1st edition of this book was published (1996) there have been many changes. Sandy, bless her little canine heart, passed away at the age of 23. Some of the folks I wrote about have left the camelid business while others have parted from their mates and some have died. I have re-married and re-located.

Some things have stayed the same. Alliteration is still playing a part in my life. I married a man by the name of Brad Bennett on the 22 of May of 1999 and honeymooned in Bora Bora! Our dog's name is Rocky Raccoon...it is kinda spooky.

Brad and I have just settled down in Bend, Oregon after spending almost two years on the road in a motorhome. I don't think I could have even dreamed that one up eight years ago! My next book is going to be titled "Motorhoming as a Metaphor for Marriage!"

Re-reading the text of this book I realize that despite the passing of time and the many changes in the lives of the players, the lessons I wrote about in this little book are still the same and still just as meaningful. This year marks my twentieth anniversary as a teacher of camelid handling. Alpacas are more popular than ever and grace the cover of this, the second edition. Llamas, despite a bit of a hiatus in popularity, are experiencing a renaissance. And me, I am still teaching folks about their animals and busier than ever.

Here's to these wonderful camelid companions ... I look forward to seeing you around the paddock!

Have the courage to be a little crazy

THIS BOOK
IS ABOUT

This book is about llamas and alpacas. Not what they eat, their history, how to raise them or what you can do with them. It is a book about what they do to you and for you. Why those people who love them can't seem to get enough of them. Why their owners feed them, take care of them and worry about them. Why lives are changed to include llamas and alpacas, and why people go to such lengths to keep them. Open your heart and these mysterious creatures will teach you about life in a way all their own. As we live and walk this earth experiencing successes and failures, disappointments and challenges, we learn and we grow. Often lessons are learned from our fellow man. It is difficult, however, given our competitive nature and pride to accept criticism and correction from our fellow human beings. People who have learned to give well-timed and appropriate feedback in a way that it can be accepted and understood represent the outstanding teachers and managers of the world. The animals in our lives are also our teachers. They are direct and they call it how they see it when they see it. They are not always kind, sometimes abrupt, but they offer their lessons without judgment.

I enjoy alliteration. Even after I was divorced, I kept my married name of McGee. There is certainly nothing wrong with my maiden name of Willis, but I had become so attached to the rhythm associated with the double "M" that it was either keep Marty McGee or change my first name to Warty. In keeping with my alliterative tendencies I have created and compiled a list of Camelid Characteristics and words that come to mind when I think of camelids. These captivating and clever creatures not only keep us calm, cool and collected and teach us about cooperation. They also bring to our lives comedy, contentment, congeniality, companionship, calmness, charm, charisma and comfort.

I am presenting this topic from two perspectives. I lived with Perry McGee on our 72-acre property we named Zephyr Farm in up-state New York from 1982 to 1992. I was on hand for births, deaths, sicknesses and the incredible racing around the pasture that happens at sundown that, try as you might, you can't explain to someone who hasn't witnessed it! I did heat waves, cold snaps and rain ... I thought would never stop. I helped pound the ice out of water buckets, sat up with sick llamas all night, struggled to bring the hay in before the rain and in the midst of what seemed to be diabolically-timed mechanical difficulties. I have stayed home when I didn't want to waiting for babies that didn't come when they were supposed to; and for some that never came! I have run outside to see the newest baby struggle to his feet and his feet and his feet and his feet...

Try new foods

After leaving Zephyr Farm
in 1992, I traveled continually.
I connected with animals
vicariously, watching and
helping other people with
their creatures. The contrast
of my life as a gypsy
with my visits to dedicated
animal lovers truly illustrated
the magic of living with
and loving animals ...
particularly camelids.

In addition to my own years of llama experience, I have visited llama and alpaca enthusiasts the world over. It doesn't seem to matter whether you are from New Zealand, Australia, France, England, Switzerland, Germany, Canada, or Maryland, if you are susceptible to the camelid "thang", it cuts across cultural differences.

I have often wondered what it is that attracts some people so strongly to llamas and alpacas. It is certainly not their willingness to lick your feet, as often as not, llamas and alpacas prefer their people not even get close to them. I make my living traveling around teaching people how to behave in a way that these aristocrats of the animal world find non-offensive. These dedicated camelid enthusiasts pay the property tax, buy the food, deal it out, pick up the poop, pay the vet bills and then pay me money to go to a training clinic about how not to offend them. Go figure. What is it about these creatures that inspires this love, loyalty and magic? Why do people go to such lengths for their llamas and alpacas? Money? There is not money enough to justify sitting up night after night with a dying llama. There are few things more agonizing than to attend to a baby that may or may not make it. Money does not enter in to these situations; something else takes over, our appreciation for the will to live—an equal appreciation of a graceful death. Llamas and alpacas lend dignity to both and from them we learn.

Camelids teach us to live
in the moment. It isn't as if
they don't have a past
or can't remember things
that have happened in the
past, they do not dwell
there. The past is only
important as it pertains to
the present.

CAMELIDS
TEACH US

I find that when I truly connect with an animal and establish a bond, I must crawl inside the moment with them. The bills, the mortgage and other responsibilities must be put away for a time. Sitting in the field or the barn and communing with your camelids does something to time. Time doesn't actually stand still, but it ceases to be the tyrant that it often is. I once met a llama person who told me that he put a couch in his barn. He would go outside, sit on the couch and play the violin, and the llamas would gather around to listen and always stayed until he finished. Because I make my living teaching people to understand their camelids, I spend as much time as almost anybody thinking about the way they think. I have come to appreciate how marvelous living in the moment can be. Colors are brighter, sounds are more compelling. I think part of the reason people gravitate to any thrilling sport or scary movie is the ability to make the past and future go away. Llamas and alpacas do it naturally all day, every day, and by living and working with them, you can learn it too. It is not the destination, it is the journey.

Color doesn't make a difference

EXPERIENCING THE EARTH MOVE

Why is it, do you think, that some humans go ga ga over camelids? I say some because camelid nuts are rather a select group. Have you noticed that not everyone is blessed with this particular idiosyncrasy? I have actually seen people walk up to a llama or an alpaca, say something like "That's nice, do you eat them?" and walk off, not experiencing the earth move. I just shake my head. They just don't get it. For those of us who do get it, IT JUST IS. We really don't need to pick it apart. I will never forget the first time I saw a group of llamas. The nearest I can figure I became aware of llamas when I read an article in the Smithsonian magazine in 1980. The article mentioned that llamas produced valuable wool. I thought it would be fun to investigate another wool animal. I went to see a herd in Pennsylvania that was advertised in the magazine. After a three hour drive, I can remember hopping out of my little pick-up truck, walking up to the fence and falling love. It didn't matter if they had wool or feathers, I knew the moment I saw them they were going to be a part of my life.

Don't be timid...
Hair is an extension of your ego

◄ Good fences make good neighbors

MORE HONEST THAN WORDS

I think it is a marvelous cosmic joke to make an animal as beautiful and elegant as the camelid and then make it so it prefers not to be touched by just anyone. Aloof and suspicious, they stifle our efforts at affection and insist on doing things their way. Then to top it all off, Mother Nature gives them the ability to spit—and on top of all they can choose how to spit. Our little camelid buddies can do the air spit or they can do the grain spit or the infamous no-holds-barred (luggee) spit. I don't know of anything that makes a person angrier quicker than to be spit on by another person. Spitting is about the worst, most insulting thing one human can do to another. So when llamas and alpacas spit on us, it pushes all the buttons that create a wonderful scenario for learning lessons about life. We learn self control and self-examination. We learn about taking responsibility for provocative behavior. We also learn that our bodies are often much more honest than our words. Camelids know this and so do our fellow humans, on a conscious as well and uncon-scious level. They call us on our real motives and attitudes, and they do it fairly and squarely. I spent some time in the army in what seems now like a different lifetime and certainly like life on a different planet! I was on my way home from a hard day at the "war" dressed in a tight fitting army skirt, pumps, a dress shirt with all the silly do-das the army insists you put on and wearing the most ridiculous hat ever invented. I didn't like being in the army and I particularly didn't like being in the army that day. I am driving along in my little car heading toward an overpass. I glance up and see two young boys, maybe thirteen years old or so leaning over the edge of the overpass. Everything seems to slow down. It's as if my consciousness has left my car and I watch the scene from above. I see the car head toward the overpass. I read their little boy minds and I see them bring up their "cud" and spit. I see the car and the "luggee" head toward each other. I hear the music reach a fever pitch just as spit connects with the windshield. WUMP! I am back in the car. Quick as a bunny I turn on the wipers and smear the disgusting thing all over the windshield. I lose control. I slam on the brakes, pull the car over and before I can get hold of myself, I am climbing through the underbrush up the bank in my panty hose and black pumps. To this day I can still see the looks on the faces of those two. As I lock eyes with them about halfway up the bank, they turn and run and I come to. I really wasn't sure where I was. I was scratched, bleeding and muddy. That was the first time I was ever spit on.

Dirt is a good thing

Sometimes it's good to keep
a low profile ▶

A TALL POPPY TALE

Fast forward. I have lived and loved camelids now for years and have learned a few things. I am down under teaching the morning of my first llama and alpaca training clinic in Australia. I have already taken a bit of good-natured Aussie joking about my training methods. I really want to wow these folks. Just before lunch they bring out "Mother Superior." Mother, as she is affectionately called, is a huge llama imported from South America and now living with Max and Nancye Moore. The importation process is not a easy one and Mother has learned to be a fighter and a screamer. Her post importation approach to handling of any sort, benign or otherwise, is to continually scream and spit. Max dutifully explains Mother's approach to humans more for me than for the group; they already know about her! I begin my routine with Mother and she does great. I am satisfied. The group seems impressed. I start to take off the halter when someone from the group asks a question. I turn my back to Mother and earnestly begin to answer the question. Mother caught the "finished vibes" and, when I didn't follow through with the release, decided she'd had enough. She quietly came up from behind and spit. Now I have to go into a bit of detail on this; she not only spit on my head, she spit in my ears. It was so runny it ran down the side of my face and onto my shirt. She fired off about ten rounds and then hung her head and began to scream. I can only imagine how much self control it took for this gal to participate for the first magical ten minutes without relying on her habitual patterns. I told her I was done and I didn't let her go. She did the best she could for as long as she could. I deserved what I got. I let her out of the catch pen and faced the group - spit faced we might say. I did my best to explain what had happened. Thankfully it was lunch time and I could absent myself to clean up and regroup.

Was my first day my last and would I be the laughing stock all over Australia? Australians have an expression - "tall poppy syndrome." A tall poppy is a person who holds themselves above everyone else much the same as the lone poppy that sticks its head up above the others. If I had done a perfect job with Mother Superior I would have been a tall poppy - pleased with myself and set apart from everyone else. As it turned out, Mother Superior did me a great favor. Everyone understood exactly what happened, saw my mistake and certainly did not discount the good work I did with "Mother". It was funny. I became a part of the group. The story made the grapevine rounds like wildfire becoming legendary and probably did a better job of clinic promotion than any number of advertisements. When someone asks me, 'Do llamas and alpacas spit?' I answer, 'Yes, thank goodness!'

Have a hobby

Always ignore geese

I am going to do you, the reader of this book, a very big favor. I am going to give you cosmic reasons to the age-old question of WHY LLAMAS and WHY ALPACAS? I lived in Santa Fe. You may have heard that Santa Fe is now the new-age capitol of the world. There is an astrologer, channeler and massage therapist on every corner. You can even get a massage in the grocery store. No Kidding. Since I lived in Santa Fe, my thought patterns have strayed into the cosmos. I think I may have been a llama before. Anyone who looks at the length of my neck or the size of my ears thinks llamaesque. I can do the eye thing and the clucking like I have done it in a past life. I have been told more times than I can say that I look like a llama. By the way, I consider it to be a compliment.

WHY LLAMAS?
WHY ALPACAS?

So, no need for mundane answers like llamas don't ruin the trail, they can carry a third of their body weight or you can spin an alpaca's wool. Of the thousands of camelids in the United States, how many see the business end of a pack? How many have actually provided a sweater's worth of wool? How many alpacas can pay themselves off with their wool clip alone? Don't get me wrong here; I appreciate all the stuff llamas and alpacas do. I spin and weave and pack, but I also know that there is something else at work. Hang onto your reading glasses, we are going off into the profound here. Perhaps this book will help you when you have to explain to your in-laws why you sold your comfortable house in the burbs near the great school for the kids, took off the sculptured nails, quit the bridge club and decided that there is something really special about cleaning up paca poo. "Mom, people actually sell it, really."

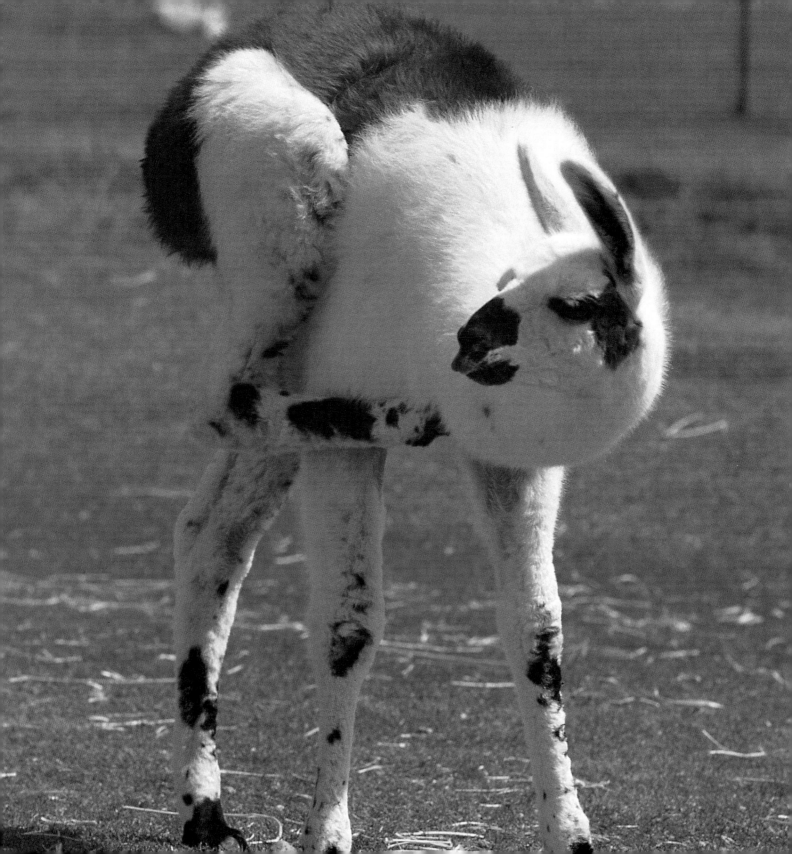

◀ Scratch when it itches

If you can't reach it
get someone to help you!

Llamas and alpacas
teach us to appreci-
ate independence
... we learn to wait,
we learn not to
push the bounds of
intimacy too soon,
and we learn not to
reach out and grab
at things without
being invited.

Try a new approach

THE
ALLURE

Part of "the allure" can be explained by a camelid's hard-to-get nature. I know that we are straying into the dog versus cat thing here. I wrote an article about cats and camelids a few years ago and I was amazed at the similarities not only in temperament and personality but physically. Just one example: cats and camelids are both copulation-induced ovulators and breed in essentially the same position. In any case, cat people understand the concept of sucking up to an animal. What have you really accomplished when your dog likes you? Most dogs like everyone. As a casual weekend guest walking in the door from the airport, I get the same overly enthusiastic greeting that the owner gets. Let's face it, most dogs are pretty easy. And what do they get for their undying devotion? A lot of the time they get pushed away and ignored, but whenever you want them, they are there. So we take them for granted. On the other hand, how do you feel when your cat decides to sit in your lap...you let your legs go numb and your bladder burst before you get up. Llamas and alpacas know the same secrets cats do. Never, never, never pander to a human. What can we as human beings, particularly women, learn from this ironic state of animal affairs? I will tell you what we can learn...being hard-to-get works. Women out there, take a life lesson from your llamas and alpacas.

The secret to allure isn't just being the most beautiful. If you want attention from a man, behave like a camelid. Don't make it your mission in life to please him. Please yourself. Be aloof and casual. No big deal if he calls – it's probably a good idea to be busy most of the time. You are doing him a favor by allowing him to approach you! Men, if you want the woman of your dreams, don't try to corner her. Come on too strong and it feels like a trap. Independence is attractive whether you are a person or a camelid. Llamas and alpacas show us that chasing, grabbing and holding lead to evasion. Stand on your own, have patience and the formerly elusive will often come stand next to you.

▲
◀ Exercise daily

LIVING WITH
YOUR ANIMALS

Sometimes at the end of a clinic the group gathers in a circle to offer comments about the weekend and discuss what they have learned. I remember one clinic in particular. It seemed like everything went really well and as each person contributed their thoughts, I was feeling good about things. A very stern looking gentleman raised his hand and stared hard at me and said, "I think you have misrepresented yourself!" I could feel the color rise in my face and my stomach knot up. I couldn't speak. Then he said, "You told us this was going to be a llama training clinic and it's not ... it's a people training clinic!" He then broke into a big grin. The group laughed with him. This comment really hits the mark.

Llamas and alpacas have taught me the truth in adage, "The only behavior you can change is your own." You can tie an alpaca, repeat a training sequence over and over until a llama finally gets it, or you can drag them into a trailer or over an obstacle. You can make a llama or an alpaca tolerate just about anything, but you can't make them like you. That is a decision that is completely up to them. If you would like your llamas and alpacas to want to spend time with you, you have to work on yourself and your approach to living with, training and managing your animals.

People new to llamas and alpacas are always vaguely disappointed when they reach out and this beautiful seemingly touchable animal moves away. Llamas and alpacas can keep themselves slightly out of reach dancing just at the end of our fingertips. This is just the way they are ... or are they? When I first met llamas and llama people, I was told repeatedly that llamas don't like to be touched, especially anywhere near the face. I accepted all the conventional wisdom with nary an "are you sure?" I accepted these limitations, did things the way I was told and my llamas acted just as they were "supposed" to.

Animals come with instintive responses that serve them in their natural environment. They will opt to run first - "the flight response". If that doesn't work, they struggle to get away - "the fight response." And if that doesn't work, they will stop, being very still or go limp - "the freeze response". In cases of extreme fear, some will lose consciousness - "the faint response". Many people believe that animals are limited to this repertoire of instinctive responses. I haven't found this to be true. Having a readily available instinctive response doesn't mean an animal can't think. What I have found is that a frightened animal reacts instinctively and has trouble thinking. The same is true of humans. Have you ever had a performance anxiety? Most humans can't think straight when they are nervous or afraid. Humans are also creatures of instinct and react instinctively when they feel fear. Flight, fight, freeze, faint responses are very much human.

Keep your ears open

Be kind to those that are different ▶

LISTENING TO YOURSELF

The way I learned to catch a camelid was to haze it, ease it or chase it into a corner. Next, I would cut off any escape route by sticking my arms out and lunging back and forth. Eventually I moved closer, grabbed the animal around the next and held on. Most llamas and alpacas will eventually learn to stand compliantly in the corner and allow a human to complete the haltering process. Many camelids also learn selective obedience; that is, if you are a good-sized llama and you are dealing with a smallish person, you don't have to go along with the training program.

After learning to consider how really intelligent all animals are and to put myself into their point of view, I suddenly realized exactly why my llamas stayed at the ends of my fingertips. They never knew when my arm would go crazy and "act out," so better to keep themselves at arm's length. How could they relax around me when they never knew if I would reach out, grab them and hold them against their will? I abandoned the corner-grab-hold technique, began using a catch pen and grain incentives, and found my llamas experiencing a complete change of attitude. They no longer got ready to run when I entered the barn. They began to let me touch them. They would actually invite it. I eventually discovered that most llamas love to be scratched on the back and some enjoy a belly rub. My llamas didn't dislike being touched; they disliked being cornered and held. Using training techniques designed to minimize fear and create opportunities for thoughtful behavior allowed the animals to bloom and grow right before my eyes.

The more I lived and worked with llamas and alpacas the more I began to realize how much physical, mental and emotional attitude affected my animals. Animals rely on their ability to read body language. The next time you work with an animal, pay attention to your balance and breathing - you can be sure that your animal is highly tuned in to these indicators of your attitude. Most people inhale and then hold their breath when they concentrate ... just before bearing down with toenail nippers, sliding the halter over the nose, squeezing in the eye medicine. Holding your breath and tightening your body indicates non-verbally that something bad is going to happen and creates anxiety in the animal. Why is it that some people seem to have a magical way with animals or with people? Because the person inspires confidence and makes the object of their attention feel safe. What makes a person appear confident? It is mostly non-verbal. It is carriage and breathing and balance. Animals can help you learn how to be confident. The animals in your life can become your very own biofeedback loop. Listen to them and they will help you learn to listen to yourself.

Make someone feel better
just by being there

◀ It's okay to be confused

BUTTERMILK

Many times llamas and alpacas become a mirror for what is an issue in your life. I tend towards being a control-oriented person and not surprisingly, I also have issues with authority. My tendency is to resist a rule I don't understand simply because it is a rule. As you might imagine, I had big trouble in the army. I often meet camelid control freaks who hate to follow rules they don't understand. When these problem animals come to a training clinic, I can pick them out as soon as they walk into the pen with me. These camelids might be presented as difficult to halter or lead, but the basic problem is the traditional approach to animal training. An intense fear of being controlled will make them fight any attempt at dominance. They are very bright so repetition bores them into acting out. These types of animals occur in all species. In the dog world, they are called the alpha dog and in horses, the rogue horse.

Bill and Jackie Mathis brought five llamas to a clinic I gave in Texas, one of whom I will never forget. I really don't think Bill wanted to be there and it took a lot of effort to round up these wild llamas and get them in a trailer. But their good friend Emily Klauss was hosting the clinic, and Bill and Jackie wanted to offer a good show of support. The llamas arrived on Friday night before the clinic, and I was on hand when they were off-loaded. I watched as the first four bolted off the trailer. The last animal was a large white female. She walked up to the edge of the trailer, had a look around and stepped out. I usually like to begin with the animal that is the most difficult. As it turned out the large white llama, "Buttermilk", the last out of the trailer, was known as a three-man llama. She was the most difficult to handle, she fought the halter like a crazy person and had hurt people who had to work with her. I had a feeling about Buttermilk. I didn't think she was the kind of llama who was difficult because she lost control and couldn't think. I thought she was a llama that couldn't stand to be forced. She had to have a level of participation and understanding or she would be unreasonable. I remember Bill saying that he didn't want me to get hurt and I promised him that I wouldn't take any chances.

I entered the pen with Buttermilk. I maneuvered her into a rope instead of cornering her. I offered her some food and I let her move away from me within the confines of the pen when she wanted to. Buttermilk moved maybe twice and when she figured out that I wasn't going to hold her, she never tried to move away again. She stood there like a perfect lady and let me halter her two or three times. Bill and Jackie couldn't believe their eyes and half jokingly asked if I had given her drugs. Buttermilk, like all of us, needed to feel safe. Some people feel safe in a structured environment with rules; others are uncomfortable with rules they don't understand and can't help but fight them. Knowing who is who is the secret.

Treasure your friends

Share secrets

A LINE
IN THE DUST

When I am having trouble dealing with a person, I reflect on what llamas and alpacas have taught me about approach behavior that leads to acceptance rather than fear. I think about not trapping my fellow human into my point of view and the value of providing an escape route. I concentrate on my breathing, staying in balance - physically, mentally and emotionally. I reflect on how important it is to be reasonable and to give a person time to think about what it is that I am asking. Breaking down complicated tasks into smaller manageable bits and allowing the animal time to think about things and make sure it feels safe to proceed are useful people tools as well. Llamas and alpacas have also taught me that whether you are working with an animal or a person, approval, acceptance and positive reinforcement work much better than judgment, force, intimidation and repetition.

Having spent a lot of time teaching animals and people, and having been a person for almost 40 years (and perhaps a llama before that), I have just about decided that the huge gulf that people know exists between humans and animals is a lot less distinct than we think. I have noticed that animals think a lot more like we do than we think they do. I have also noticed that humans, me included, react instinctively a lot more than we think we do. Llamas and alpacas have taught me a lot about how I deal with my own fear, and how to recognize and deal with fear in other people. Most of the difficulties people have with other humans are related to fear, instinctive responses and lack of thoughtful behavior. Confrontation often provokes instinctive reponses. I have always thought of myself as a person who would not let fear stand in my way. Animals have taught me that although I didn't run or freeze, I often fought without thinking. I always thought there were only two ways to react to confrontation. When a fellow human or an animal dares you to cross a line in the dust, you back off and do what is the equivalent of the submissive crouch or you puff yourself up, react in kind and escalate the encounter. Animals have taught me there is another option. You can decline to play the win/ lose game. You can choose to ignore the line and simply refuse to be manipulated into the competition.

Stand up for what you believe

Be joyful in the season ▶

CHUPEDERO

It is 1987. I am new at training and am anxious to appear confident. My host, at my request, assembled some challenging llamas for me to work with at this, my first public appearance as a trainer. I have learned many lessons in life. One is not to ask someone to assemble difficult llamas for you if that is not exactly what you want. Some of my llama students at this – my first clinic – included a llama who had to be anesthetized in order to have his halter adjusted! This llama drags a thirty-foot lunge line at all times because once he gets loose, you can't get any closer to him than that. My host also managed to find the two largest bottle-raised geldings I ever saw in my life, both of whom were people-aggressive. She also found a massive gelding named Chupedero (not his real name) that was a former public relations llama now clearly on strike. To say his owners had problems loading Chupedero is an understatement. It took a couple of helpers several hours to load him and the spit flew freely. The whole loading scene was very unpleasant for everyone, especially Chupedero. Everyone involved needed a second shower that morning – arriving very late and in quite a state. As a youngster, Chupedero would jump in a van, wow the nursing home residents and the school kids all day, tackling stairs, linoleum, hospital rooms and an other obstacle that came his way. Sometimes Chupe visited two or three places a

week. At about eighteen months of age, he began loading reluctantly and finally refused to load at all. He had to be folded
up bodily and put into the van. Then he began to spit, bolt and
rear while on his visits. He wouldn't get back in the van to
return home without a scene. His owners were completely
flumuxed. They couldn't figure out who stole their wonderful
boy. They were truly frustrated. They had tried just about every tactic they could think of and were obviously doing the best
they could.

It's okay to stare unabashedly

◄ Be mysterious

Based on the description of his behavior, I thought Chupe was started too soon and then overworked. His initial behaviors indicating the beginnings of adolescent burnout were missed. He was forced to cooperate and then punished for acting out - standard human approach to dealing with animals. My idea was to work him over some easy obstacles to regain his cooperation around loading. My ego can be a problem - particularly when I am being watched by 35 pairs of eyes. I had planned an obstacle session for Chupedero; he decided it would be a lesson in humility for me. He began by cooperating. The obstacles we were playing around with were chicken feed for a llama with so much experience. At the beginning of the session he walked over some plywood, but at the end of ten minutes he wouldn't walk over a pole on the ground. The longer I worked and the harder I pressed him, the more recalcitrant he became. I was beginning to get very embarrassed, but I began to understand this guy. In order to get Chupe to trust me, he needed to know I would be willing to back off. All of my conventional conditioning around animal training cried out, "MAKE HIM DO IT. FORCE HIM. YOU HAVE TO WIN!" On the other hand, I knew where that tactic was likely to take us - to the showers! Time for some spin control. I explained to the audience that Chupe was asking me if I was listening. He wanted to know what I was going to do if he didn't cooperate. His behavior had nothing to do with fear of the obstacles; his fear was of me and my control. Rather than fall on my proverbial sword over a pole on the ground, I decided to abandon the obstacles and try something completely different. We did some easy leading without obstacles. I massaged his mouth and ears, encouraged him to relax and called it quits. I felt all kinds of mixed emotions from the audience. I am sure many thought I rewarded him for misbehaving and that I allowed him to win. I didn't think of it that way. I was more interested in creating a possibility for him to trust me.

Chupedero had to go home and at the end of the day, so, of course, I offered to help load him. I am now thinking to myself, "There surely had to be an easier way to make a living." Almost everyone decided to stay for the "loading show." As I led Chupe over to the awaiting step-up trailer, people got busy rounding up some items I thought might be helpful: poles, bales of hay and plywood for a makeshift ramp. Other folks were busy setting up their lawn chairs for what they thought would be an interesting experience. Chupe followed me to the trailer and jumped right in – he never hesitated a step. Sometimes not pressing your point is the best way to make it.

Appreciate a good dog

School uniforms are a good idea

BOYS AND GIRLS

It is true. Boy camelids are from Mars and girl camelids are from Venus. My first five baby llamas were girls and the next six were boys. Of course, I watched every move the darlings made at first and I assumed that all baby llamas played like the girl babies I was watching. I never had a chance to watch boys play regularly until I had lived with llamas for two years. I was amazed at the difference in play behavior. The boys played so much harder and they did different things. Chest butting, leg biting and neck wrestling are not the strict province of male babies, but little boys certainly take it a lot more seriously.

Before I was a llama owner and watcher, I never had much of an opinion about whether or not girl and boy humans are socialized to be different or if we are born that way. Do little girls like dolls and not trucks because they are expected to or is it in our genes? If animals are any indication, some of it must be inborn. Certainly we are more than our chromosomes, and it is important to be able to choose our own path, but I don't find it insulting to recognize and honor my inborn tendencies.

I can't help but think of sports bars and football games when I watch the boy llamas pacing themselves silly, walking the edges of their territory and making a big show of pooping and peeing just so. Watching the girls sort out who is the boss lady is a study in subtlety. The angle of a nose in the air, the turn of a shoulder, the set of a jaw, indicates who is who in the girl pastures.

The Zephyr Farm herd grew slowly from a small group of three breeding females. Talara was the oldest when the triumvirate was assembled and so was the natural leader of the group. As the herd grew, she remained boss lady. We eventually sold Talara to Jamie Miller and Jim Smith in New Hampshire. Talooloo who had been second in command moved into the vacant spot. Talooloo had a more rigid management style, but everyone accommodated themselves to the change. All remained peaceful until Talara came back to Zephyr Farm for breeding. I will never forget watching her disembark. She jumped out of the truck, took a thorough look around and marched over to the prime spot at the feeder, displacing poor Talooloo who stood there in disbelief. It was fascinating to see the interplay be-

Maintain your dignity
even under difficult circumstances

tween the two women llamas. Talooloo continued to reluctantly defer to Talara and the rest of the llamas fell into line. Talara stayed for about three months and went back home to New Hampshire to live. Talooloo breathed a big sigh of relief and resumed her duties.

Talara came back again the next year and the same drama played itself out yet again. Talooloo was crestfallen for a few days, muttered a lot under her breath and went along with the program. The following year when Talara came back, things changed. During Talara's absence the herd had grown. When she arrived again there were a significant number of females living at the farm that had never met Talara and didn't know her as the former boss woman. She jumped off the truck, sauntered over to displace Talooloo and it didn't happen. Talooloo held her ground. The rest of the llama group stopped eating to watch the drama. Talara and Talooloo did the nose in the air thing, then they swapped spit. They backed off, glared at each other and then reared and bumped chests. It was the fight of the century. We never figured out who won. That evening it appeared to be a standoff, but as the days went by it was clear

what had happened. We now had two groups of llamas where there had been one before. We had the old-timer group who remembered Talara and chose to align themselves with her; then we had the new crew who only knew Talooloo as the boss and remained loyal. The two groups alternated territory. One group would take up residence in the barn and the other group would hang in the field. Then as if there had been an official changing of the guard, they would swap places. The two groups stayed as separate as if they were fenced apart. The youngsters played together, but the adult females stayed in their chosen group.

Talara came back again the next year and her influence was gone. It was sad to see her get off the truck and join the group, as one of the group. She never made an attempt to resume her place of pre-eminence. Then again, she was the undisputed boss at her farm in New Hampshire. Perhaps she found three months of going with the flow to be a welcome rest from the rigors of management.

Be nice to the new kid

Rest when you're tired ▶

Question authority

◀ Be tolerant

BODY
LANGUAGE

Being non-verbal, in our sense of the word anyway, animals are a perfect example of action speaking louder than words. Working with camelids has taught me to watch and pay close attention to body language in both humans and animals. When I say something I guess will be new and perhaps controversial, I look closely at the assembled group. I can see the arms fold, hear the intake of breath and see the crossing of legs. I can also see and appreciate it when folks nod their heads, lean forward, sigh and relax their shoulders when they are interested and fully engaged.

I was standing by the door of the barn scratching Talooloo's back when Betty came up rudely and pushed Talooloo aside to get some back scratching of her own. I couldn't believe it. Talooloo was getting very pregnant and her velvet management glove turned into an iron fist around this time of her pregnancy. Instead of slitting her throat, Talooloo responded to Betty without so much as an upturned nose. I scratched Betty for a while and wandered into the house scratching my own head. What was going on? I thought it would be a good idea to watch the gals a bit closer to see what was amiss. I began to notice that Talooloo was spending a lot of time lying down. She was eating okay, but she would eat lying down, reaching for grass with her long neck without getting up. Then she would stand up, move to a new spot and immediately lie down again to resume eating. After a day or two of watching this we called our veterinarian to have her checked. Sure enough a rectal exam confirmed that she had a uterine torsion. Lying down took the pressure off her insides. She was not too uncomfortable to go off her feed, but she sure didn't feel like defending her place in the herd. We planned an attempt to untwist her, but she must have heard us plotting and fixed it herself, delivering a big healthy boy a month or so later.

Have a taste for the unusual

◀ Be a good listener

AN EXCELLENT ADVENTURE

As adults, we get wrapped up in life's responsibilities. We don't play, we don't explore. We try sports and even then we gear up and take our chosen sport so seriously that it ceases to be play and becomes something very much like work. Let your animals remind you about what it is like to experience real adventure: To boldly go where you never gone before not knowing what you will find.

I am sitting in the living room when Perry bolts by wearing nothing but a towel and a look of terror on his face. "What is wrong?," I insist as I follow him at a dead run in the direction of the barn. He yells over his shoulder, "I think I left the gate open." Perry and I had lived with and raised llamas and sheep. They both have wool. That is where the similarity begins and ends. Llamas have a sense of adventure. Sheep are wonderful in their way ... adventurous they ain't. If you leave a gate open it might take the sheep a week to notice. Not so with camelids. An open gate is an invitation to explore. In a new pasture they leap, run and cavort like it is a wonderful new planet they just discovered.

It is now maybe an hour before sundown. Eleven llamas including a brand new baby are nowhere to be found. Our llama field joins a neighbor's 100-acre pasture – a magical open plain of lush grass sure to captivate and occupy any self respecting llama. Of course, that is where they will be. Perry and I run up the hill, breathlessly scan the pasture and real panic begins to set in. There is not one llama out there! Perry suggests that I go home in case the llamas come back or we get a phone call from a neighbor. He will grab some grain and go scouting. I am a woman of action. Send me around the countryside searching but don't send me home to wait — Chinese Water Torture! I go home and call the police. The desk sergeant stammers when I call and ask if anyone has reported finding eleven llamas. I stay home as long as I can. I can't stand it and head out to see if I can find the llamas. I look for signs of the llamas, or Perry for that matter. NOTHING. I arrive back home. I am trudging back to the barn when I hear Perry yelling to open the gate. I rush to the barn and the group of ELEVEN are heading home. When llamas are really excited they walk as if on high heels. These llamas had a really spectacular time, they were barely making contact with the ground.

Later sipping a drink and relaxing on the porch Perry filled me in on the "capture." Ignoring the hundred acres of grass, they crossed a dirt road through a neighbor's field into a secluded pasture and settled down for the night. The odd part was as soon as they spotted Perry and knew they had been found, they got up and headed home. The jig was up. Perry never had to lure or herd them. They ignored the grain and passed Perry by looking like errant teenagers caught on a joy ride.

Be supportive

But not overly accommodating

Don't worry so much about your appearance ▶

EXPECTING THE UNEXPECTED

Animals can teach you to believe in the divine, serendipity, to expect the unexpected and to take it as it comes. It is 1993. I have been teaching training clinics for six years. I have been there and done both this and that. I am becoming perhaps a bit blasé about how things are going. I am teaching a clinic at Dale and Mike Pettigrew's ranch in Colorado. We have a good turnout including a bunch of interested veterinary students from Colorado State University. The students are new to camelids and Dale has promised them a farm tour after the clinic is over. Dale and Mike had purchased a young male named Matterhorn at auction and found out later that he had a very severe heart defect. He would not be used for breeding nor would be ever be able to carry a pack or handle much stress. They were told he would probably die before he was four since his heart would never be able to handle adult weight. Dale and Mike dearly love llamas and loved this male. They decided to let him live out his life as normally as possible. Matterhorn lived in the male group, played and sparred, and had a great time. At the time of the clinic, Matterhorn is just about to turn four and Dale has decided that he would be much more comfortable without a full fleece weighing him down. She would like to shear him with as little stress as possible. Enter Marty.

Dale has asked if I would shear this llama as part of the clinic weekend. I agreed and we planned to do the shearing at the end of the first day. As luck would have it, we ran out of time on the first day and decided to shear first thing in the morning when it was cool. The class departed for dinner on the town, the vet students stayed for the tour and I headed into the house for a glass of wine. I heard my name being called. It sounded urgent so I ran outside, looked to the barn (trying not to spill my glass of wine) as I ran to see what had happened. The group had gathered around a brown form lying still on the ground. Following an afternoon of grazing and cavorting with his mates, Matterhorn had collapsed and died, a bit like dying on the golf course. I drained the glass of wine in one gulp. Now, I can tell you I was very sad that this llama had died and ... I was ecstatic that he decided to do it on his own time and not in the catch pen with me shearing him. Every time I closed my eyes for days afterward, I would see imaginary headlines in every llama publication: **Marty McGee Murders Llama with Hand Shears. Thirty witnesses watch in horror as McGee delivers the coup de grace.** Sometimes seemingly related events really aren't. Timing is everything.

Llamas and alpacas teach us that good things are worth waiting for and working for. Their friendship must be cultivated carefully. It takes time for a llama or an alpaca to trust. Their trust is hard won, easily lost and well worth the effort.

Be inscrutable

THE SHOW MUST GO ON

Animals don't waste a lot of time agonizing over things. Watch a camelid give birth and you gain an appreciation for understatement. Alpaca and llama mammas are virtually unflappable. They set about this remarkable task with little to no fanfare. They will often graze as the new baby slides to the ground. Animals seem to take things as they come without a lot of unnecessary drama. They keep their feelings to themselves. Herd managers must hone their powers of observation; critically ill camelids will often show nothing more than a lack of appetite. Working with animals has taught me the value of keeping my head in an emergency and keeping my feelings to myself when it is appropriate. I have learned to keep on going; knowing that I can fall apart later if need be.

I arrived in Georgia in time to share a dinner with Jim and Liliane Grant, Diane and Lance Bell and their dog, Sandy. I was conducting a training clinic at the Grants. Two fun couples, a sweet agreeable dog and a wonderful evening. At the time Sandy was a grand ol' dame of fifteen, slow moving and close to deaf, but still quite a presence. During dinner Lance and Diane share a few Sandy stories. She is a tiny thing about the size of a small terrier; sixteen point three pounds according to Lance. They found Sandy near starvation under a rock with a broken hip. Lance asked the vet what kind of dog she was and he said, "She is a dog and that is as far as I will go." She is to the Bells the most wonderful dog in the world. They seldom go anywhere without her — Sandy has stayed at some of the fanciest hotels in the country.

The evening before the training clinic the Grants house was full so I borrowed Jim's car and headed to a hotel in nearby Cartersville. The next morning I showed up at the farm to prepare for my class. Lance directed me past the parking lot for the clinic participants and up to the house. Liliane and Diane were in a golf cart and waved me to a parking spot near the house. I eased the car up glancing at Liliane and Diane for directional conformation and saw their faces change from smiles to abject horror. Diane leaped out of the golf cart and ran toward the front of the car. I never saw Sandy, and being deaf and slow she probably didn't see or hear me. I put the car in reverse and then slammed it into park. The next moment was one of the worst in my life. I jumped out of the car not wanting to see what I had done and fearing the worst.

When I got out of the car, I could see that Sandy was still in the land of the living. I couldn't tell if she was hurt or not. No blood, moaning or yelping, but she was very still. It was an unbelievable relief to see her breathing. Everything sped up and began to swirl around me. Diane rushed off with Sandy in her arms. Liliane ran to call a vet; someone else rushed to get Lance and I was left alone standing by the car, perhaps experiencing the worst moment of my life thus far.

Whenever possible, spend the holidays with loved ones

I made my way toward the barn and my waiting students. I had to get myself together and teach a clinic in about half an hour. The show must go on. I passed Lance rushing up the hill from the parking lot holding his chest. He said frantically, "Someone has run over our dog." As I shrunk down into the earth, I could hear myself say, "Lance, I am the one who hit Sandy. I am pretty sure she is going to be okay." I continued on to the barn and tried to compose myself. All I really wanted to do was collapse in a heap. I think I truly understood what the word mortified means. Diane had gone to the vet. The preliminary report from Al Tollefson, a veterinary technician on hand to attend the clinic, was encouraging. Lance stayed at the clinic and like the veteran he is, introduced me to the group as planned. He sang my praises and opted not to mention that I just ran over his dog. So.... I told the group what had just happened. Lance and Diane are very well liked and almost everyone knows of the devotion they both feel towards Sandy. I didn't know if I would be lynched; I did know it would be easier for me to carry on if the class was aware of what was going on.

Amazingly, I did a pretty good job of the morning although periodically I stared off into space and forgot what I was doing. Just before noon Diane and Sandy returned from the veterinarian; Sandy with an amazing bandage on her left hind foot and Diane with a look of relief. Four of Sandy's toes had been broken. Apparently I caught her foot under the front tire — she was going to be fine. The rest of the day went by in a blur of happiness. I was on cloud nine. The Bells would accept no money or my offer of free training for the rest of their lives. That evening after dinner we were making logistical plans for the next day. I mentioned that I didn't need the car again and could get a ride back to the hotel. Jim Grant, always ready with a joke said, "Oh go ahead and take the car. I have already alerted all the humane societies and veterinary clinics between here and Cartersville!"

I drove slowly and very carefully back to Cartersville thinking how lucky I was that this all turned out so well. After I drove about five miles down the road I began to feel strange. I began to hyperventilate. I couldn't get my breath and I had to pull over to breathe and cry for awhile. I believe I was experiencing something akin to a post traumatic stress attack. I think we all do what we must, and our bodies and minds help us out until there is an opportunity to fully experience an event. Sandy is now eighteen and hanging in there.

When all else fails, go fishing

◀ Accessorize

TINGO

Tingo was my first llama. In 1984 we were both still trained in the old school. I knew Tingo didn't much care for being touched, that is just the way llamas are. I only had two llamas at the time, so Tingo was a breeding male, packer *and* public relations llama, like it or not. I can't remember exactly what kind of event it was now, maybe an alternative farm day or a county fair. Lots of people, lots of noise, lots of kids and lots of questions. "Hey do those things lay eggs? How many in a litter? What are they good for? Do you eat 'em?" and, of course, the every popular, "Do they spit?" It is late in the day. I don't know about Tingo, but I am tired and cranky. Tingo has been standing in the middle of his 12x12 pen all day and has refused to let anyone pet him. He watches the humans as they reach through the panel trying to cop a feel. Periodically he looks over at me as if to say, "Get me out of here and you haven't heard the last of this!" I haven't insisted that he put up with a bunch of fondling. I figure good public relations begins with honesty; people may as well know that most llamas don't let most strangers pet them. I don't feel it is a human right to touch everything just because we want to and Tingo agrees.

I glance up and watch as two people supporting an adolescent boy between them make their way down the aisle to Tingo's pen. The boy is wearing a protective helmet. He is clearly disabled. His helpers walk him up to the pen and he leans on it. Tingo walks over and greets this young boy with a sniff and stands quietly with him for several minutes. The boy doesn't have much control over his movements. He almost grips and punches rather than petting. Tingo doesn't seem to mind. He stays patiently until the boy leaves and then resumes his place in the center of the pen.

photo courtesy of CAROLYN BLALOCK

View crabbiness as an art form

Remember your beginnings ▶

OF UNICORNS AND CAMELIDS...

Llamas leapt out of the back of a pickup truck and into my heart in the fall of 1982. I remember those first weeks like it was yesterday. I walked to the barn each morning in complete amazement that there were llamas there to greet me. One morning I walked in to see my precious girl llama standing around miserably with her mouth hanging open shaking her head and coughing. She must have just finished telling her mate in no uncertain terms that she was pregnant. At the time I thought she had been poisoned. I called the vet and obviously before she could get there the problem had disappeared. I will never forget what a kick it was to walk those llamas out and about in the neighborhood answering all the inevitable questions with what was, as I look back now, a remarkable amount of misinformation. We watched for months for the first baby, finally turned our back for an hour one morning and the next thing we know...there she was.

Twenty years later, camelids are still a wonderment. I still find it inspiring to stand close to a llama or alpaca, to feel their soft lips on my cheek and to gaze into their eyes. Being with llamas and alpacas is truly the closest you can come to knowing a unicorn and still stay in this world.